MAYA

SECRETS *of their* ANCIENT WORLD

Justin Jennings, Martha Cuevas García,
and Roberto López Bravo
with a contribution by David Pendergast and Elizabeth Graham

Royal Ontario Museum Press

EXHIBITION FLOOR PLAN

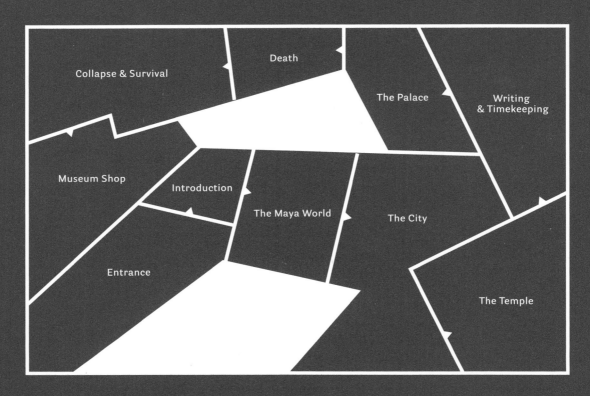

Collapse & Survival

Death

The Palace

Writing & Timekeeping

Museum Shop

Introduction

The Maya World

The City

Entrance

The Temple

CONTENTS

FOREWORD

Upon publication in the early 1840s, English artist Frederick Catherwood's watercolours of the Maya ruins captivated the western world. These images of ruined cities, deep in the jungles of Mexico and Central America, conjured an advanced ancient civilization, long overtaken by the natural world. The Maya's achievements in architecture, astronomy, calendrics, commerce, sculpture, technology, and writing systems reached astonishing heights. The allure of their world persists through time.

The Royal Ontario Museum is delighted to partner with the Canadian Museum of Civilization in hosting the blockbuster *Maya: Secrets of their Ancient World*, a remarkable exhibition highlighting this ancient Mesoamerican civilization's Classic Period (250 to 900 CE). As visitors journey into the heart of a great ancient Maya city, they will unveil many of the mysteries of this legendary civilization. In collaboration with Mexico's National Institute of Anthropology and History (INAH), the ROM and the CMC have brought together some of the greatest artistic and cultural achievements of the Maya civilization. The exhibition features nearly 250 artifacts, including sculptures, ceramics, masks, and other precious works, many of which were associated with Maya temples and palaces.

Maya: Secrets of their Ancient World is the result of an international collaboration between Canada and Mexico. The ROM's Justin Jennings and the CMC's Jean-Luc Pilon have joined with two Maya archaeologists from Mexico: Martha Cuevas García and Roberto López Bravo, in curating the show. The exhibition explores life in the royal courts, revealing the relationships that connected Maya rulers to each other, their followers, the environment, the cosmos, and the passage of time. Visitors will also learn that unlike other ancient civilizations such as the Aztecs, the Maya civilization was never an "empire" unified by a single governing body. Instead, numerous independent city states, sharing similar traits, practices, and beliefs, were all considered Maya. The Maya developed astronomy, as well as a complex calendar system and an elaborate writing system. They were also known for their highly adorned architecture, such as temple-pyramids, palaces, and observatories.

We are also pleased to include a special section in this publication on the Royal Ontario Museum's very significant contribution to Maya archaeology, including former ROM archaeologist Dr. David Pendergast's discovery of one of the great treasures of ancient Maya civilization.

As always, we are indebted to Louise Hawley Stone, a celebrated ROM patron, whose lasting legacy to the Museum includes two endowed curatorial chairs and the Louise Hawley Stone Charitable Trust, which funds strategic acquisitions and publications. This essential guide to the exhibition is a product of her foresight and generosity.

We would like to thank the following for their support in bringing the world of the ancient Maya to the people of Ontario, Canada, and beyond: Exhibition Partners—the Canadian Museum of Civilization, the Instituto Nacional de Antropología e Historia, and the Consejo Nacional para la Cultura y las Artes; Supporting Partner—the Government of Mexico; Promotional Partner—GO Transit; Media Partner—the Toronto Star; and Government Partner—the Ontario Cultural Attractions Fund. Because of their passion and commitment, we are privileged to present a truly great exhibition.

Janet Carding
Director and CEO
Royal Ontario Museum

Portion of *La Casa de Las Monjas*, Uxmal, watercolour, Frederick Catherwood (1799–1854)

INTRODUCTION

In regard to the age of this desolate city I shall not at present offer any conjecture . . . The trees which shroud it may have sprung from the blood of its slaughtered inhabitants; they may have perished howling in hunger; or pestilence, like the cholera, may have piled its streets with dead, and driven forever the feeble remnants from their homes . . . One thing I believe, that its history is graven on its monuments. Who shall read them?

— John Lloyd Stephens, describing the Maya site of Copan, Honduras, in *Incidents of Travel in Central America, Chiapas, and Yucatan* (1841)

Stela at Copan

By the time the Spanish Conquest of Mesoamerica began in 1517 CE, the great cities of the Classic Maya civilization had been abandoned for more than five hundred years. The tree-clad temples and toppled sculptures in these ruins were largely local curiosities until the mid-nineteenth century, when the best-selling accounts of John Lloyd Stephen's and Frederick Catherwood's travels ignited widespread interest in the ancient Maya world. Like earlier visitors to these sites, Stephens and Catherwood were overwhelmed by the grandeur of Maya art and architecture. Who built these sites, they asked, what was their culture like, and why did they leave? Each year, archaeologists, epigraphers, and ethnologists come closer to answering these and other questions. Yet, many secrets from this ancient world remain to be uncovered.

Answering who built these cities is as simple as looking at the people who now live around these sites. The Maya are not a vanished people—today there are some ten million Maya individuals bound loosely together by their shared cultural and linguistic heritage. Extending over an area roughly the size of California, the Maya world encompassed coastal swamps, lush jungles, arid plains, and high sierra on lands found in present-day Mexico, Belize, Guatemala, Honduras, and El Salvador. The roots of the modern Maya can be traced back in this region to at least the first villages, which were settled by around 1200 BCE. As population increased, sites grew in both size and complexity,

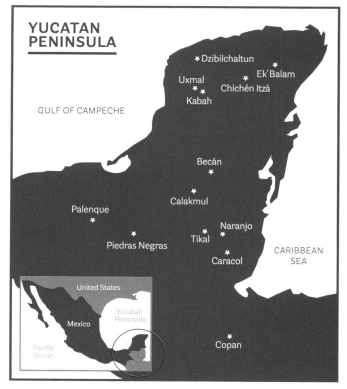

Major Maya cities

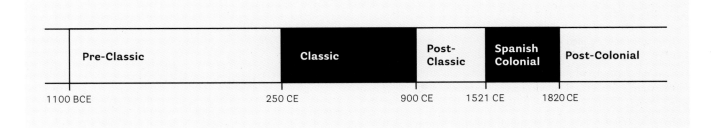

| Pre-Classic | Classic | Post-Classic | Spanish Colonial | Post-Colonial |

1100 BCE   250 CE   900 CE   1521 CE   1820 CE

Chronology for the Maya Region

and by 500 BCE the Maya world was already dotted with pyramids, elite residences, and elaborate tombs. The largest buildings ever constructed by the ancient Maya were built by the first century CE at cities such as El Mirador in Guatemala. El Mirador's tallest temple, "La Danta," is one of the largest pyramids in the world, rising approximately 70 metres above the surrounding forest.

Maya: Secrets of their Ancient World showcases the Maya of the Classic Period (250–900 CE), an era of incredible artistic and intellectual achievement rooted in institutions that had developed at earlier sites such as El Mirador. Classic Maya society was organized around royalty living at cities such as Calakmul, Tikal, Copan, and Palenque. The cities were thinly spread across wide areas, so portions of a city would have had a farm-like feel with crops, fruit-bearing trees, and domesticated dogs and turkeys surrounding the house platforms that ringed the more monumental sections of the city. A visitor coming to town would have been joined by farmers walking to their fields and porters bringing goods on tumplines and in backpacks to the site's lively marketplaces. One might have heard the din of a limestone quarry in the distance, and caught the aroma of tree resin being burned as incense in a nearby ceremony.

Those privileged enough to walk up the steps into the royal palace and wander through its rooms and patios would have seen a wide variety of domestic, administrative, and residential activities. Paintings and carvings from the period provide us with a window into life at the royal court. We see rulers sitting cross-legged on thrones greeting dignitaries from other cities. Musicians and dancers are shown entertaining nobles, while scribes—many of whom enjoyed the highest social ranks—are depicted bent over beaten bark paper, painting glyphs with sure hands. In other scenes, nobles share a cup of frothy, unsweetened chocolate, a dwarf holds up a mosaic mirror made from pyrite, and a woman in a diaphanous gown places a pot of maize gruel on a servant's head.

From the palace, one would have seen soaring pyramids that were capped by temples. Some temples were dedicated to the patron deities of a specific site. Palenque had three of these gods; another site, Dos Pilas, had two. Depictions of local gods on temples were joined by references to gods that were shared across the Maya world such as the Sun God, K'inich Ajaw, and Chaahk, the Rain God, and by depictions of venerated ancestors whose souls likely dwelt in the sky. The gods and ancestors possessed *k'uh*, a vital essence that kept the world functioning properly. By their special connections to the divine, Classic Maya nobles also possessed *k'uh*—it oozed from their palms and was carried in their blood—and they regularly participated in small private ceremonies in palaces and temples to maintain their link to the sacred. Other ceremonies were elaborate public events where elites dressed in incredibly ornate costumes and even personified the gods for crowds of people who congregated in the central plazas.

Daily life mural from Calakmul

This somewhat idyllic portrait of a visit to a Classic Maya centre, however, is incomplete. Warfare, torture, and sacrifice were also fundamental aspects of city life. Cities were in conflict with each other, and warriors returning with booty and bound captives would have also been an occasional sight in the plazas of Maya cities. These captives were often nobles, even kings, and they could be held by a rival for years. Since their blood contained the vital essence *k'uh*, these elite prisoners were sometimes bled and occasionally killed as offerings to gods and ancestors. Bonampak's Temple of the Murals, for example, depicts a grisly scene in which the ruler Chaan-Muan presides over the open-air torture of warriors recently captured in battle. Blood drips from mutilated hands, and a severed head rests on a bed of leaves. For much of the Classic Period, this violence was often related to the occasional clashes between Tikal and Calakmul, two superpowers who dominated large parts of the Maya world. By the beginning of the tenth century, however, these two cities were in decline and the region descended into increasing warfare.

It is important to understand that a city's temples, plazas, ball courts, and palaces were built not just for the elite. They were also meant to attract farmers, traders, craftspeople, and other groups to live in or frequent the city. Classic Maya rulers probably had limited control over the people who lived outside the palace. Since farmsteads were widely dispersed beyond the

Reconstructed mural from Bonampak

Temple of Inscriptions at Palenque

city centre, elites likely had only weak control of agricultural production. The few goods that a family could not make at home were usually provided by local craftspeople or trading partners. People were highly mobile. They could, and sometimes did, just walk away from a city that had lost prominence. Yet, they usually settled back down again near another urban centre. If most Maya got so little from those living in cities, then we might wonder why people offered their time, labour, and sometimes even their lives to sustain the opulent lives of royalty.

There were in fact many reasons. Some cities created large reservoirs that helped farmers make it through the dry season, and the cities provided public entertainment such as spectacular performances in ball-game courts and great plazas. Yet, the biggest reason behind the prosperity of Maya cities was the belief

Temple of K'uk'ulkan at Chichén Itzá

that they were the *sancta sanctorum* of the Classic world, and the duties performed by the rulers and their courts were essential for life. Maya royalty spent much of their time legitimizing their rule by demonstrating their intimate connections with gods, ancestors, and the cosmos in general. The Long Count calendar, for example, was often used to tie current leaders to important events in the deep past. Royal astronomers searched the sky for the auspicious scheduling of events, and rulers sacrificed their own blood as offerings to the dead. To a significant degree, the masterworks of Maya art and architecture were created as justification of sacred rule.

By the beginning of the ninth century, confidence in the royalty was slowly waning. Instead of John Lloyd Stephens' almost apocalyptic scenarios for the end of Copan that begin this guide, the Classic Maya collapse was a century and a half decline spurred on by a myriad of factors that included overpopulation, increasing warfare, environmental degradation, drought, and shifting trade routes. The glyphs provide only a few hints of the final power struggles, but the targeted destruction of symbols of power in some cities suggests that the ultimate end of Maya royalty may have been fuelled by a crisis of faith—were the Maya an increasingly desperate people who no longer believed that their rulers had special links to the divine? With the exception of a few squatters who lingered for a few more decades, the Maya people melted into the countryside and the abandoned architectural centres were swallowed up by encroaching forests.

The end of many Classic Maya cities, of course, did not mean the end of the Maya. Uxmal, Labna, and Ek' Balam on the northern Yucatan Peninsula briefly rose in prominence during the ninth century, but these were overshadowed during the tenth century by the rise of Chichén Itzá. The site, a blend of Maya styles with elements from central Mexico, became the largest city of its time in Mesoamerica. The complex symbolism of sacred rule that permeated Classic Maya art, however, was gone. Post–Classic Period iconography suggests both a shift away from the concentration of power in a single ruler and the state worship of K'uk'ulkan, the feathered serpent. Chichén Itzá was in decline by the end of the eleventh century, and another site, Mayapán,

eventually took its place as the major power of the Post-Classic Maya world. By the time the Spanish conquest of Mesoamerica began in 1517 CE, the precarious political unification of the eastern Yucatan Peninsula had shattered into sixteen rival states.

Protected in places by an almost impenetrable wilderness, the last of the Maya were not brought into the Spanish Empire until 1697 CE. The conquest shattered many long-standing Maya traditions. Classic Maya culture, having been re-shaped by elements introduced during the Post-Classic Period, was now more radically altered by the addition of Christian and Spanish ideas. Cattle, pigs, and chickens were introduced, new saints and sacraments transformed religious life, and the Roman alphabet replaced glyphs. Despite all these changes, critical aspects of Maya culture have endured and the echoes of the Classic Maya can still be seen in today's Maya communities. The languages that they speak, the ritual calendar that they follow, and the striking profiles of their faces represent just a few of the connections between the present-day Maya and their ancestors.

Maya school children in Tenejape, Mexico

THE EXHIBITION

Maya: Secrets of their Ancient World tells the story of the ancient Maya through almost 250 objects from the Classic and Post-Classic periods. Most of these come from Mexican museums, though there are also artifacts from museums of the United States, Canada, and Great Britain. The exhibition includes some of the most famous examples of Maya art, but also boasts many objects that have never previously been displayed in a museum. Most of the artifacts in the exhibition were found during the course of archaeological excavations, and a few—including a beautiful low-relief panel from Palenque—were reconstructed especially for this exhibit.

The exhibition is organized as a journey through the countryside and into the heart of a Classic Period Maya city. We begin by exploring the lush, diverse environment of the Yucatan Peninsula and learn about the critical role of farmsteads and agriculture. Much of our time, however, is spent wandering the city. We enter a plaza and learn about the ball game, fashion, and food before going through the door of a temple façade to find objects that speak to the Maya conception of the cosmos. The culture's enigmatic glyphs are then decoded, as is the unique Maya calendar system, which has ignited unfounded doomsday scenarios around the year 2012. We enter a palace and behold the presence of royalty; burial masks and other funerary goods help us to understand the Maya concept of death. The exhibition ends by addressing the Classic Maya collapse, the rise of Chichén Itzá, and the survival of the Maya to the present day.

In the pages that follow, some of the objects in the exhibition are used to illustrate aspects of the lives and beliefs of the ancient Maya. We hope that the guide, as well as the exhibition itself, inspires you to learn more about this early civilization. This guide is not meant to be exhaustive—the data on the Maya are extensive and ever-changing. Each year new discoveries are made, and each year new secrets are revealed. We encourage you to treat this guide as the beginning of a life-long journey through the intricacies of the Maya world.

THE OBJECTS

A Powerful Beast

Lidded bowl depicting a jaguar
Ceramic
Early Classic Period (250–600 CE)
Yucatan Peninsula, Mexico
Museo Regional de Yucatán Palacio Cantón, Mexico
10-631820

The wide variety of animals depicted in Maya art reflects the diverse environments found in the Classic Maya world. Animals, however, were also often associated with the divine and believed to have supernatural powers. This lidded bowl depicts a jaguar, a fearsome predator and a symbol of death, darkness, and the underworld. When warriors went to battle they identified themselves with the jaguar, and even the Sun God took on aspects of the jaguar during his nightly journey through the underworld. It was the unique privilege of rulers to use the skin, claws, or head of the jaguar since the animal was the guardian of royalty. Rulers were therefore often depicted wearing a headdress, cape, loincloth, or sandals made from jaguar skin. Though we do not know where this vessel was found, it was likely recovered from a tomb since depictions of jaguars were common in funerary assemblages.

Ducks and the Soul

Lidded bowl depicting a duck
Ceramic
Early Classic Period (250–600 CE)
Becán, Campeche, Mexico
Museo Arqueológico de Campeche Fuerte de San Miguel, Mexico
10-568668 0/2

This lidded vessel was found among a rich group of offerings in a funerary chamber at Temple IX at the site of Becán. The top of the lid is modelled into the form of a duck's head, while the duck's wings are incised into the body of the lid. The ancient Maya linked animals to different aspects of the sacred world through their particular behaviours and habitats. The jaguar, for example, was associated with death and the underworld because it was a nocturnal hunter. Aquatic and raptorial birds were associated with the watery underworld, the place where people went when they died. Ducks were considered to be souls of the dead and celestial messengers, and it was believed that gods took the form of ducks as they journeyed between the sacred mountains and the sea. Ducks were also considered to be the bearer of seeds in agricultural fertility rites.

Maya Portraits

Among the ancient cultures of Mesoamerica, the Maya are distinguished by their authentic portraits of important people. Some of these portraits decorated the façades of palaces and the tombs of important rulers, while others were used to remember deceased family members and were kept inside the houses of noble families. For exterior portraits, the material most often employed was stucco, a paste made by combining lime, water, and sand. The smaller portraits made to be kept in homes were more often fired from clay. Maya portraiture usually shows men and women in the prime of life. Depictions of children were rare, and depictions of the elderly were generally only those of gods, especially the Creator God, Itzamnaaj. These portraits give the modern viewer a sense of the dental and cranial modification practised among the ancient Maya, as well as the hairstyles and headdresses they wore.

**Head of a woman wearing an elaborate
   flower headdress**
Ceramic
Late Classic Period (600–900 CE)
Tenam Rosario, Chiapas, Mexico
Museo Regional de Chiapas, Mexico
10-338430

Head of man with a headdress
Stucco
Late Classic Period (600–900 CE)
Palenque, Chiapas, Mexico
Museo de Sitio de Palenque Alberto Ruz L'huillier, Mexico
10-458670

Face of a man with scarification
Ceramic
Late Classic Period (600–900 CE)
Comalcalco, Tabasco, Mexico
Museo de Sitio Comalcalco, Mexico
10-575760

Dressing the Part

Whistle in the form of a standing man with a tall headdress
Ceramic
Late Classic Period (600–900 CE)
Yucatan Peninsula, Mexico
Museo del Camino Real de Hecelchakán, Mexico
10-343354

Social status among the Maya was marked in part by their clothing and personal adornments. The basic dress of men was a loincloth, while women wore a dress. People of all classes wore jewellery, such as earrings and lip plugs. The costumes of nobles were more elaborate—a pair of jade mosaic ear spools might be added to an ensemble, or a blouse could be richly embroidered. Figurines recovered from funerary offerings on Jaina, an island off the coast of Campeche, show people from a wide spectrum of Maya society. This figure depicts an important dignitary who wears a necklace with large beads and a high hat that was likely made from paper and cloth. At Palenque, portrayals of individuals wearing cylindrical hats similar to this one were of high-ranking priests who participated in royal succession rites.

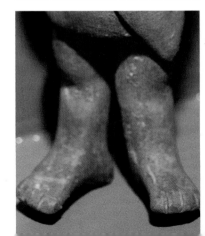

An Earful

Pair of ear spools with incised glyphs
Obsidian
Early Classic Period (250–600 CE)
Altun Ha, Belize
Royal Ontario Museum, Toronto, Canada, on loan from the
    Government of Belize
L965.9.78A & B

Ear ornaments were such a fundamental part of Maya dress that their replacement with strips of paper was a symbol of captivity and defeat. Nobles preferred flaring ear spools made from jade and shell. The wearer inserted the smaller end of the spool into a hole in the earlobe that had been gradually expanded since childhood. A tubular plug was then often placed through the hole in the spool for stabilization. These fluted ear spools were found in a richly furnished tomb of a middle-aged man at Altun Ha. The spools are made from polished obsidian, a material rarely used by Maya jewellers since it is extremely difficult to work this volcanic glass into such shapes. The ear spools were likely an heirloom—the glyphs give a person's name and title in a style that predates the burial itself by a century.

Exotic Chocolate

Lid of a pot depicting a monkey with cacao pods
Ceramic
Late Classic Period (600–900 CE)
Toniná, Chiapas, Mexico
Museo de Sitio de Toniná, Mexico
10-569388

To make chocolate, the ancient Maya fermented, dried, and roasted the bitter beans of the cacao tree. The beans were then ground up into a paste and mixed with water, cornmeal, chili peppers, and other ingredients. Cacao was perhaps first domesticated by the Olmecs (1500–400 BCE) in the Soconusco region of the Pacific Coast in Chiapas, Mexico. The tropical trees are difficult to cultivate, and the beans were a highly desired long-distance trade good throughout much of ancient Mesoamerica. Cacao (*kakaw* in ancient Zoque, the language of the Olmecs) was added to the wide variety of fermented corn drinks consumed by Maya elite during festivals. This whimsical lid probably depicts a spider monkey, an animal known for its great appetite for cacao, wearing a collar of the tree's pods. Sitting upon a now lost jar, the monkey would have jealously guarded the precious cacao seeds that the vessel likely held.

Precious Jade

Plaque engraved with glyphs and an image of a noble
Jade
Late Classic Period (600–900 CE)
Altun Ha, Belize
Royal Ontario Museum, Toronto, Canada, on loan from the
 Government of Belize
L966.10.1

A prized trade good, jade was symbolically connected to life because its colour mirrored water and vegetation. This example from a tomb at Altun Ha is one of the largest known jade plaques from the Maya world. One side shows a ruler seated on a throne that depicts the head of the Sun God. The vine-entwined cacao tree rising behind him likely represents the World Tree that linked the heavens, the earth, and the underworld. The throne sits on top of the Witz Monster, a living mountain where the gods dwelt. Twenty glyphs on the other side of the plaque refer to a conquest and enthronement that occurred in the late sixth century CE. Since the jade was carved some fifty years before it was placed in the tomb, the plaque was probably an heirloom passed from father to son.

Booming Drums

Drum
Ceramic
Late Classic Period (600–900 CE)
Yucatan Peninsula, Mexico
Museo Arqueológico de Campeche Fuerte de San Miguel, Mexico
10-624218

Music was an important part of Maya life. The range of instruments included conch shell trumpets, long wooden trumpets, ceramic drums, rattles, flutes, and even turtle shells that were banged with antlers. Recovered from the site of Calakmul, this drum is notable for its large size. Covered over tightly with a piece of deer hide, the drum would have made a deep booming sound when banged with the hands. Depictions on murals and pottery show that each royal court likely boasted its own orchestra and dancing troupe that performed on a wide variety of occasions. A scene from the Temple of the Murals in Bonampak, for example, shows a long procession of musicians during a celebration of a military victory, and painted ceramic vessels often show groups performing in front of a ruler on a throne.

A Cosmic Game

Ball-player figurine
Ceramic
Late Classic Period (600–900 CE)
Campeche, Mexico
Centro INAH Campeche, Mexico
10-339776

In Classic Period Maya mythology, the stars descended into the underworld each night to battle and defeat the forces of darkness. The triumphant stars rose each morning, thus ensuring that life on earth would continue. For the ancient Maya, ball-game courts were portals to the underworld; as such, they were places of death but also of resurrection. The courts that often graced Maya centres were ritual spaces within which humans could participate in the ongoing struggle of life over death. The ball's flight from one end of the court to the other symbolized the movement of the stars. This figurine's elaborate headdress, as well as its padded yoke and votive axe (both worn around the waist), underline the ritual importance of this game. Although fraught with cosmological significance, the ball game was also a recreational sport played away from the confines of the courts.

Warfare and Sacrifice

Figurine of a captive
Ceramic
Late Classic Period (600–900, CE)
Yucatan Peninsula, Mexico
Princeton University Art Museum, Princeton, U.S.A.
Gift of Gillett G. Griffin
2003-148

The Maya ideal of combat was a heroic face-to-face battle between opponents wielding spears, clubs, and axes. One of the goals of warfare was to capture an opponent—an action referenced in the glyph *chuhkaj*, "he is seized/roped." Though some captives were dispatched on the field of battle, many were taken back as trophies by the victors. Captured warriors were generally represented alone with their arms bound and stripped of their clothes, ear spools, and other insignia of rank. Captives were often presented to rulers, humiliated, mutilated, and eventually sacrificed. Prisoners are frequently shown grimacing in pain and pleading for their lives, but the portly noble depicted in this figurine seems to be facing death with dignity. The fish barbels, scalloped eyebrows, and false beard that adorn the man's face seem to suggest his transformation into a supernatural being, and perhaps allude to his impending sacrifice by fire.

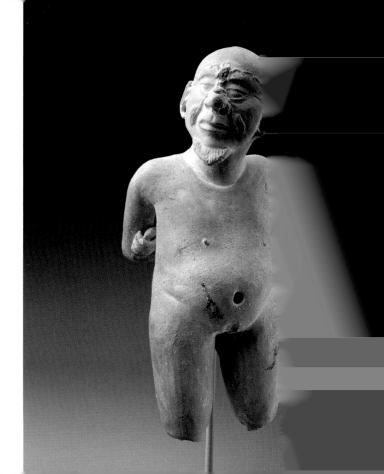

A King Captured

Sculpture depicting Palenque's ruler, K'inich K'an Joy Chitam II, as a captive

Sandstone
Late Classic Period (600–900 CE)
Toniná, Chiapas, Mexico
Museo Regional de Chiapas, Mexico
10-409956

The site of Toniná featured many depictions of captives that had been brought to the city. This sculpture stands out from the others, however, because the figure remains unbound and he retains much of his jewellery. Most significantly, the captive wears a Jester God headdress, an insignia of royal office. The glyphs on the figure's leg identify him as K'an Joy Chitam II, the ruler of Palenque, and the glyph to the right of his leg suggests that he was captured by Toniná in 711 CE. The two cities had been battling for years. The date 711 CE also marks the beginning of a dark decade in Palenque's history since we have no more glyphs from the city until Ahkal Mo' Nahb III ascended the throne in 721 CE. The capture of K'an Joy Chitam II did not result in his death. Instead, he somehow eventually managed to make his way back to Palenque.

The Hero Twins

Plate depicting the resurrection of the Maize God
Ceramic
Late Classic Period (600–900 CE)
Petén Basin, Guatemala
Princeton University Art Museum, Princeton, U.S.A.
Museum purchase, Fowler McCormick, Class of 1921, Fund
    1997-465

The *Popol Vuh* is a seventeenth-century book that describes the adventures of the Hero Twins, Hunahpu and Xbalanque, before the creation of the current world. As the story begins, the twins' father, the Maize God, is killed on his way to play a ball game against the gods of the underworld. His head is hung in a tree, and he impregnates the daughter of one of the underworld gods by spitting into her hand. After the Hero Twins are born, they decide to travel back to the underworld to avenge their father. They use their cunning and ball-game skills to survive trial after trial, and eventually they kill the underworld gods, resurrect their father, and rise into the heavens. This Classic Period vessel demonstrates the antiquity of core aspects of this myth by depicting the resurrected Maize God emerging from a skull seed (a symbol of death and rebirth). The four other figures are likely the Hero Twins and their monkey half-brothers.

A Monster Slain

Lidded bowl depicting an iguana-jaguar slaying humans
Ceramic
Early Classic Period (250–600 CE)
Becán, Campeche, Mexico
Museo Arqueológico de Campeche Fuerte de San Miguel, Mexico
10-568677 0/2

The lid of this bowl found in Structure IX at Becán features a scene
that likely alludes to a myth in which the slaying of a reptilian
creature allows for the creation of the earth. The scene is dominated
by the depiction of an animal that combines the features of an
iguana with those of a jaguar. The creature's jaws gape open to
unleash a torrent of blood, which comes in part from the corpse
of a person that has been chewed in half by the iguana-jaguar.
The remains of two other mutilated victims, one wearing a lizard
headdress and the other a peccary headdress, can be found on either
side of the creature. The animal's triumph was likely short-lived.
From its jaws, one can see emerging the head of the Creator God,
Itzamnaaj, who may be killing the iguana-jaguar from the inside and
forcing it to disgorge its victims so that they may live again.

A God of Plenty

**Capstone depicting the god K'awiil carrying a sack
   of cacao beans**
Paint on limestone
Late Classic Period (600–900 CE)
Yucatan Peninsula, Mexico
Museo Amparo, Mexico
52 22MA FA 57PJ 1465

The capstones located at the top of Maya corbel-vaulted buildings
were sometimes painted with scenes. In many cases, the god K'awiil
is depicted, usually in association with food, especially corn and
cacao, and often with a pile, sack, or basket of grain. Associated
with royal power, sacrifice, abundance, and fertility, K'awiil is often
shown with his foot in the form of a serpent. In this example,
K'awiil runs or dances while carrying a bag of cacao beans. The
glyphs on the bag literally read "nine eight-thousands." Since "nine"
in Maya languages is often used to mean "many," the glyph is likely
being used to emphasize that the god is carrying a great quantity
of food. This interpretation is supported by another glyph on the
capstone that reads *ox wi'il*, meaning "an abundance of food."

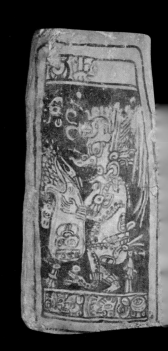

Bloodletting

Stingray spine with an incised hieroglyphic text
Stingray spine
Late Classic Period (600–900 CE)
Xicalango, Campeche, Mexico
Centro INAH Campeche, Mexico
10-170208

Autosacrifice was one of the most important rituals of the Classic Maya because the offering of one's own blood could be used to make contact with gods and ancestors. People from across the social spectrum performed autosacrifice, but the blood of Maya royalty was seen as a more potent gift. Stingray spines were commonly used in autosacrifice to puncture the skin so that blood could be extracted from the thigh, arms, tongue, penis, or ears. This blood was spattered on paper and then burned during rituals. In some cases, stingray spines were inscribed with the name of the owner. This example comes from the offerings in a high-status burial at Xicalango, Mexico. Some of the glyphs are illegible, and others remain poorly deciphered. Nonetheless, we can make out the following words: "in…the noble took blood (?) from the tongue… the/your sacred sky is your…shell…the chip to spear or goad."

The Vision Serpent

Doorway lintel depicting the Lady Wak Tuun speaking with an ancestor

Limestone
Late Classic Period (600–900 CE)
Yaxchilán, Chiapas, Mexico
British Museum, London, U.K.
AOA 1886-314

This lintel from the site of Yaxchilán depicts the culmination of a bloodletting ritual that likely occurred in 755 CE. Lady Wak Tuun, one of the wives of Yaxchilán's ruler Yaaxun B'ahlam IV, carries a basket that contains a stingray spine, rope, and bloodied pieces of bark paper. Another container of bloodied paper near her feet has been lit on fire as an offering to her ancestors. The smoke gives rise to a vision serpent from whose jaws emerges a human head that converses with Lady Wak Tuun. The glyphs identify the creature as a manifestation of the water lily serpent, an aspect of K'awiil, who was the patron god of Maya royalty. The lintel's celebration of the divine links of Yaaxun B'ahlam IV's family had a limited audience—only those who looked up while passing through the doorway would have been able to see the carvings.

Propitiating Ancestors

Incense-burner stand depicting the ruler K'inich Kan B'ahlam
Ceramic
Late Classic Period (600–900 CE)
Palenque, Chiapas, Mexico
Museo de Sitio de Palenque Alberto Ruz L'huillier, Mexico
10-459022 and 10-479202

Incense burners were used across the Maya world to incinerate
pom, a fragrant crystallized tree sap, and other offerings. At
Palenque, artists created particularly elaborate stands on top of
which undecorated, lidded incense burners were placed. One type
of incense-burner stand depicted dynastic ancestors who were
venerated by their descendants. The death of an *ajaw*, or ruler,
did not mean that the link with the living was ruptured. Instead,
ancestor cults maintained connections with the dead, who were
thought to work for the good of the community in the afterlife. On
occasion, the stands were portraits, and this example likely shows
the ruler K'inich Kan B'ahlam. This incense-burner stand was found
next to Temple XV, the likely funerary structure of Kan B'ahlam and
the location where members of his cult would have prayed and left
offerings. Unfortunately, the funerary chamber below Temple XV
that likely would have held his remains was looted at the end of the
nineteenth century.

Propitiating Gods

Incense-burner stand from Temple XVI with a representation of K'inich Ajaw, the Sun God
Ceramic
Late Classic Period (600–900 CE)
Palenque, Chiapas, Mexico
Museo Regional de Chiapas, Mexico
10-629763

At Palenque, there was another set of incense-burner stands that were called *ux-p'uluut-k'uh*, or god incense-burner stands. These stands were considered to be representations and incarnations of the patron gods of the city-state. Ritual life at Palenque was centred on the worship of these deities, and inscriptions describe how the god incense-burner stands were periodically replaced during ceremonies that celebrated the end of twenty-year *k'atuns* and other calendrical cycles. On these occasions, the incense-burner stands were given offerings and replaced with new examples. The retired stands were then considered "dead" and were buried on the flanks of the temples in the Cross Group. This ritual interment was practised for four centuries (450–850 CE), so there is a great concentration of these stands that remain buried in the ceremonial core of the site. To date, more than a hundred examples have been recovered. This stand portrays the Sun God as he makes his nightly journey through the underworld.

The Tools of Scribes

Paint container in the form of a curved hand
Shell
Post-Classic Period (900–1521 CE)
Yucatan Peninsula, Mexico
Museo Regional de Yucatán Palacio Cantón, Mexico
10-426205

Maya scribes used a rich variety of paints in their work and were often depicted with a paint pot in one hand and a brush or stylus in the other. In this example, an artist mimics the typical gesture of a scribe at work by turning a split conch shell into a container shaped like a cupped hand. Although only three bark-paper codices survive from the Post-Classic Period, murals, along with painted pottery, also provide windows into the artistry of ancient Maya scribes. Murals were painted by covering the limestone walls with a layer of lime and vegetal gums. The white walls were then often painted a wide variety of colours. The well-studied Bonampak murals give us a sense of how these frescoes were sometimes created. The figures were first outlined in red, and then filled in with a rich palette of as many as twenty-eight colours derived from earth pigments. The figures were then finally outlined in black.

Death of a King

Panel with glyphs commemorating the death of K'inich Kan
  B'ahlam of Palenque in 702 CE
Stone
Late Classic Period (600–900 CE)
Emiliano Zapata, Tabasco, Mexico
Museo Ventura Martín Azcuaga, Mexico
REG 2036, PM 280

In this incomplete panel, a sculptor is seated in front of a stone head
that is labelled with the glyph for *kan*, a word meaning "yellow,"
"noble," or "valuable." The sculptor holds a stone knife that is
mounted on a curved handle. This tool was used for working stone
and the accompanying inscription reads, in part, "and then he
sculpted the precious stone" (*i uxulji k'an tuun*), a stone that was
used to celebrate the end of a cycle (*laju'ntuun*). Other inscriptions
on this panel register the death of K'inich Kan B'ahlam, who died
on February 16, 702 CE, at the age of sixty-six, after ruling the city
of Palenque for eighteen years. The glyphs state that "he entered the
path," the route to the underworld. Although this panel is from an
unknown location, the content of its inscriptions strongly suggest
that it came from Palenque or one of the towns that fell within
its orbit.

End of a Cycle

Panel depicting the ruler Muyaal Hix Chaak and a functionary

Limestone
Late Classic Period (600–900 CE)
Pomoná, Tabasco, Mexico
Museo de Sitio Pomoná, Mexico
10-392507

Maya ritual acts were dictated by the calendar. Certain days in the *Tzolkin* 260-day time cycle, for example, were marked during later periods with food taboos or requirements for sexual abstinence, and people's birthdays were used to predict their destinies. The *Haab* time cycle was a 365-day year consisting of eighteen months each with twenty named days. The five extra days in the cycle were the *wayeb*, an unlucky period that was used to prepare for New Year ceremonies. Each 360-day cycle of months was a *tun*, 20 *tuns* equalled a *k'atun* (19.7 solar years), and 20 *k'atuns* equalled a *bak'tun* (394.3 solar years). By adding these cycles together into a long count date, the Maya marked time from when they thought the current world was created on August 13, 3114 BCE, in our Gregorian calendar. The ending of any one cycle and the beginning of another cycle were cause for celebration to ensure prosperity in the coming years. New stone monuments and buildings were often dedicated at the end of *k'atuns*, and each *k'atun* had its own patron deity and associated rites. This panel from the site of Pomoná

records the celebration of the end of a *k'atun* on 13 Ajaw 18 Kumk'u (9.17.0.0.0 in the long count calendar or January 24, 771 CE, in our Gregorian calendar). On the left of the panel, the ruler of Pomoná, Muyaal Hix Chaak, is depicted as he personifies and gives incense to Yax Chiht Ju'n-? Naah Kan, a serpent spirit from the waters of the underworld. To his right is a man identified by the glyphs as a subordinate ruler (*sajal*) and priest (*ti' sak hu'n*). The ceremony lasted for three days and ended on 3 Ak'b'al 1 Wayeb' (9.17.0.0.3).

See next page for illustration.

Time Altars

Altar commemorating the midpoint of a *k'atun* in 682 CE

Sandstone
Late Classic Period (600–900 CE)
Toniná, Chiapas, Mexico
Museo Regional de Chiapas, Mexico
10-460844

During much of the Late Classic Period, the site of Toniná was distinguished for both the militarism of its art and its conquests of neighbouring cities. The plazas of cities were decorated with monuments of their rulers, which were often paired with circular altars that celebrated important events such as a victory in battle, the capture of prisoners, or the completion of a ritual. The Toniná altars tend to feature two sets of glyphs. The first set, around the edge of the disk, describes the event, and the second set, in the centre, is made up of larger glyphs that record the date when the monument was erected. This altar was commissioned by Ruler 2 of Toniná, a figure called Jaguar Casper by some epigraphers, who ascended the throne in 668 CE and was vanquished in a battle against Palenque in 688 CE. The altar celebrates the completion of half of a *k'atun* in 682 CE (9.12.10.0.0).

A Life of Luxury

Cup depicting a noble gazing into a mirror
Ceramic
Late Classic Period (600–900 CE)
Greater Yucatan Peninsula
Dumbarton Oaks, Washington, DC, U.S.A.
PC.B.569

The royal court resided in sprawling, richly decorated palaces that served not only as residences, but also as reception areas, offices, banquet halls, and schools. Palace culture reached its apogee during the Late Classic, and painted vessels from this period provide surprisingly intimate portrayals of courtly life. On this vessel, a seated lord gazes into a mirror held by an attendant. The scene's small details such as the cloth and paper hanging from the wall and the bound rubber ball in the basket give a sense of how the throne room would have looked. The meaningless glyphs convey the hushed words being exchanged.

Mirrors were ascribed magical qualities in other Mesoamerican cultures, and Maya lords are often portrayed staring into mirrors. Exactly why they did so remains unclear, but it is likely that the Maya used mirrors to divine the future and to seek council by engaging with altered versions of themselves.

Banquet Foods

Bowl depicting a man drinking at a banquet
Ceramic
Late Classic Period (600–900 CE)
Yucatan Peninsula, Mexico
Museo Regional de Yucatán Palacio Cantón, Mexico
10-631806

The painted scenes on Maya ceramics are sometimes a rich source of information on daily life. This cup shows a person likely drinking at a banquet. Banquets could be public or private. They were held for a wide variety of reasons such as births, marriages, deaths, harvests, and diplomatic accords, and were often used to showcase the political, social, and economic power of the host. Some of the principal activities at these events were smoking, eating, and drinking fermented beverages to excess. Ground corn was the most ubiquitous of ingredients at these feasts—the steaming tamales, the bowls of gruel (*atole*), and the numberless cups of beer were all corn-based. Squashes, beans, avocados, and other fruits and vegetables were also common foods, while salt, honey, and peppers added flavour to the dishes. Meat, poultry, and fish were generally reserved for elite events and were cooked in stews or over an open flame.

A Turkey Mask

Figurine of a man wearing a bird helmet sitting on a blue altar
Ceramic
Late Classic Period (600–900 CE)
Palenque, Chiapas, Mexico
Museo de Sitio de Palenque Alberto Ruz L'huillier, Mexico
10-458661 0/2

This arresting figurine is notable for the quality of its craftsmanship and the conservation of its original colours. A man is shown seated on a blue altar wearing a loincloth and a helmet in the form of a bird's head. The bird is likely the ocellated turkey (*Meleagris ocellata*). Smaller and more colourfully plumed than the wild turkey of North America, this bird was associated with benevolent deities. This figurine was found among the offerings left next to two buried noblewomen in a large funerary chamber constructed below Building 3 of Group B at Palenque. The upward gesture of the figure's right hand suggests that he is a priest in the midst of a ritual act. Some specialists think that figures like these were used in divination rituals that were undertaken exclusively by women.

Ruling Women

Panel depicting a female ruler with royal sceptre
Limestone
Late Classic Period (600–900 CE)
El Cayo, Chiapas, Mexico
The Cleveland Museum of Art, Cleveland, U.S.A. Purchase from
   the J. H. Wade Fund
1962.32

Although rarely ruling in their own right, women often enjoyed
elevated status and exercised considerable power in Maya cities.
This panel from the site of El Cayo depicts one of these rare female
rulers wearing jade jewellery, an elaborate headdress, and a richly
embroidered dress. She holds in her hand the sceptre of K'awill,
god of the royal lineage and agricultural fertility. The accompanying
glyphs date from 795 CE and mention Aj Chak Wayib' K'utiim
as the ruler who ordered the woman's investiture. The woman was
likely the wife of K'utiim, who was a *sajal*, or subordinate lord,
subservient to the ruler of the nearby city of Piedras Negras. Women
rose to power only during periods of political unrest, such as when a
dynasty lacked male heirs or a standing ruler was incapacitated. We
do not know the woman's name or how she came to rule El Cayo.

The Right to Rule

Panel from Temple XXI depicting the ruler Ahkal Mo' Nahb III in a scene of dynastic succession

Limestone
Late Classic Period (600–900 CE)
Palenque, Chiapas, Mexico
Museo de Sitio de Palenque Alberto Ruz L'huillier, Mexico
10-629761

K'inich Ahkal Mo' Nahb III came to power in 721 CE during an unstable period in Palenque's history. His uncle, K'inich K'an Joy Chitam II, had been captured in battle with the city of Toniná a few years earlier, and Ahkal Mo' Nahb was likely quite young when he came to power. The trying circumstances of his accession to the throne led him to go to elaborate lengths to demonstrate his connections to gods and ancestors. One example of Ahkal Mo' Nahb's legitimization campaign is this recently discovered panel from a large carved platform in Temple XXI. The scene on the panel shows five figures in the middle of a ceremony that took place on July 22, 736 CE. At the centre of the scene is K'inich Janaahb' Pakal, the famous ruler of Palenque who had died fifty-three years earlier. Pakal wears a headband decorated with the names of two early mythical rulers, nicknamed Casper and Snake's Stingray Spine, and the glyphs suggest that Pakal's essence is fused with the earlier kings. Pakal thus represents the deep roots of Palenque royalty, and

the stingray spine bloodletter in his right hand symbolizes the blood relationships to the two figures that flank him: the reigning ruler, K'inich Ahkal Mo' Nahb III, and his brother and designated successor, U Pakal K'inich. The brothers are in the midst of a bloodletting and they are turned towards two creatures that offer them bouquets of cloth, paper, and leaves. Each creature has the head of a rat and feline paws, and wears a jaguar-pelt cape. According to the glyphs, the creatures are priests, either in costume or transformed into animal companion spirits. This and the other monuments commissioned during the reign of K'inich Ahkal Mo' Nahb III suggest that he needed to reaffirm continually his mandate to rule over Palenque. From the Temple XXI panel, we see that he was also concerned about demonstrating the sacred connections of his heir and brother, U Pakal K'inich.

See next page for illustration.

Death and Rebirth

Incense burner depicting the Jaguar God of the Underworld
Ceramic
Late Classic Period (600–900 CE)
Comitán, Chiapas, Mexico
Museo Regional de Chiapas, Mexico
10-409817

One of the more common figures depicted on Late Classic Period incense-burner stands is the Jaguar God of the Underworld, who is recognizable by the band that goes under his eyes and then twists between his eyebrows. The Sun God, K'inich Ajaw, on his nightly journey through the underworld, transforms into the Jaguar God of the Underworld. K'inich Ajaw's nightly trip to the underworld mirrored the journey taken by the deceased. For the Maya, death was a process—a several-day canoe trip with the paddler gods into the watery underworld. In some cases, royalty may have passed through the underworld to be reborn. This vessel depicts three figures from top to bottom: a seated ruler or priest dressed as the Jaguar God of the Underworld, a similarly garbed noble emerging from the head of a serpent, and the head of a jaguar. Though enigmatic, the vessel may have been used in rites to propitiate a specific ancestor.

The Face of a God

Funerary mask
Jade, shell, and obsidian
Early Classic Period (300–600 CE)
Calakmul, Campeche, Mexico
Museo Arqueológico de Campeche Fuerte de San Miguel, Mexico
10-566423, 10-566424 0/2

The site of Calakmul in Campeche was one of the most powerful of Classic Maya cities. Its tombs have provided the greatest number of burials with mosaic jade masks. Meant not only as portraits of the deceased, the masks also evoked the Young Maize God, whose resurrection led to the creation of the current world. This androgynous god was closely associated with agricultural fertility—the cycle of plantings and harvestings recapitulating his death and rebirth. The divine aspects of this mask from a ruler's tomb in Structure II-D are highlighted by the shell nose plugs and fangs. Mosaic masks were made by gluing each mosaic tile to a stucco support with tree resin, beeswax, and other adhesives. Since supports tend to decompose in the lush climate of Mesoamerica, mosaic masks are often painstakingly reassembled piece by piece by conservators.

A Final Monument

Stela incised with the last long count date recorded in the Maya lowlands (909 CE)
Limestone
Early Post-Classic Period (900–1250 CE)
Toniná, Chiapas, Mexico
Museo de Sitio Toniná, Mexico
MST 1

By the end of the ninth century, many Classic Period cities were in steep decline as a result of overpopulation, incessant warfare, environmental degradation, and other factors. As one city after another was abandoned, the tradition of long count dating came to an abrupt end. The practice of long count dating did not survive into the Post-Classic Period. This stela from Toniná contains one of the last known long count dates. The heavily eroded front of the stela depicts the city's last ruler, while the glyphs on the back of the stela read 10.4.0.0.0 or January 15, 909 CE. Toniná's royal dynasty fell soon after this date, and its palaces and temples were abandoned. Some of the city's population left the region, perhaps moving north towards still flourishing Yucatan centres such as Uxmal and Kabah. Many people, however, chose to remain. They lived in small farming hamlets, and their descendants can still be found working the land around Toniná today.

Rules of the Game

**Ball-game ring incised with a representation of K'uk'ulkan,
the Feathered Serpent**
Limestone
Early Post-Classic Period (900–1250 CE)
Chichén Itzá, Yucatán, Mexico
Museo de Sitio de Chichén Itzá, Mexico
10-290175

The ball game remained an important ritual activity after the
collapse of many Classic Maya centres. Chichén Itzá has one of
the largest ball-game courts ever built in Mesoamerica, but this
limestone ball-game ring comes from the nearby Tzompantli,
a famous structure decorated with carved depictions of rows of
human skulls that proclaim its likely association with human
sacrifice. The high-relief images on the ring show two intertwined
serpents with shells situated between them. Although the rules of
the ball game changed over time, we know that two teams tried to
pass a solid rubber ball that weighed 3–4 kilograms (6–9 pounds)
from one side of the court to the other. Depictions from the Maya
region show a ball striking heavily padded players below the chest.
Rings like this one were a late addition to the game, and a player
likely scored by putting the ball through the ring. According to
Spanish chroniclers, ball games were punishing affairs that left
players bloody and bruised.

A Reclining Warrior

Chac Mool sculpture
Limestone
Early Post-Classic Period (900–1250 CE)
Chichén Itzá, Yucatán, Mexico
Museo Regional de Yucatán Palacio Cantón, Mexico
10-569277

During his excavations in 1875 at Chichén Itzá, the explorer Auguste Le Plongeon discovered a sculpture similar to this one and named it "Chac Mool," or Red Claw, after an imagined Maya prince of the same name. Chac Mools depict reclining men with flexed knees who support raised torsos on their elbows. They tend to gaze off to the side with their hands placed on their abdomen. The figures, although only partly dressed, wear the attire of warriors. What these figures represent remains unclear, but receptacles found on the abdomen of some examples suggest that they likely served as sacrificial altars. Displaying stylistic departures from long-held artistic canons, Chac Mools are an example of the foreign influence that reshaped the culture of the Yucatan Peninsula during the Post-Classic. This Chac Mool was found inside the Temple of the Carved Columns at Chichén Itzá and is quite similar to an example known from the Toltec site of Tula in central Mexico.

Traditions Continue

Pedestal jar depicting a combination of K'awiil and Chaahk
Ceramic
Early Post-Classic Period (900–1250 CE)
Lamanai, Belize
Royal Ontario Museum, Toronto, Canada
LA 61/1

This jar was one of five vessels excavated from a pit associated with a man's burial. A pyrite mirror, a copper bell, and a shell necklace were recovered along with his remains, as was evidence of seven other long since decayed objects that are indicated only by the gold sheet that once covered them. This remarkable burial, one of forty-nine that would be eventually excavated from underneath successive floors of a structure that faced Lamanai's once bustling lagoon, was unearthed in 1974 during the first season of work at the site by Royal Ontario Museum curator David Pendergast. Found in pieces, the carefully restored jar boasts an effigy that was originally stuccoed and then painted a brilliant blue. The effigy combines features of K'awiil and Chaahk. Though K'awiil was the patron god of royalty, he shared Chaahk's association with rain and lightning. Dating to the beginning of the Post-Classic Period, the jar's effigy combines Classic Period features (an eye scroll) with new elements (a fanged mouth associated with central Mexican depictions of the Rain God).

HOW TO READ THE GLYPHS

Although many related languages were spoken across the Maya world, the glyphs were usually written in Classic Ch'oltiano, the language of the royal courts. There are almost 900 known glyphs in the Classic Period Maya writing system. About 700 of these are logograms that stand for whole words. Though some of the logograms are pictograms (they resemble what they stand for, e.g., the fish glyph), most are not (e.g., the sky glyph).

The remaining glyphs are phonetic and represent syllables. Syllables usually consisted of a consonant joined to a vowel. For example, *ha*, *he*, *hi*, *ho*, and *hu* are five syllables starting with the consonant *h*. They were written as follows:

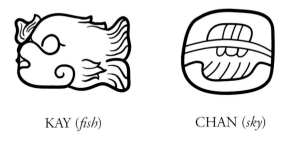

KAY (*fish*) CHAN (*sky*)

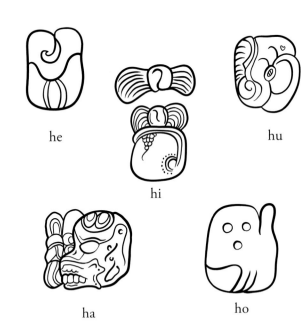

he

hi

hu

ha

ho

Words could often be written in several ways. The ancient Maya word for jaguar, for example, is *b'ahlam* and could be written in at least five different ways. Here is the jaguar head logogram of *b'ahlam*, as well as one of the ways that it was written phonetically.

Maya scribes sometimes combined two glyphs to form a completely new, single glyph. An example of this type of glyph is the combination of the syllables for *mo* and *lo*, to create the word *mol*:

B'AHLAM

b'ahlam

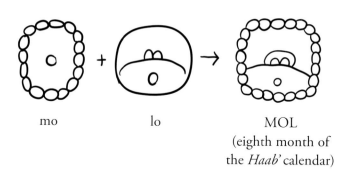

mo   lo   MOL
(eighth month of
the *Haab'* calendar)

Scribes created glyph blocks with as many as nine glyphs in order to form a word or part of a word. In general, you read the glyphs in a block from left to right and from top to bottom, as in English and French.

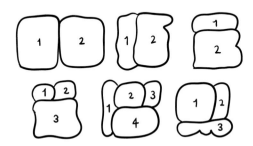

Here are some examples of reading order for more complicated glyph blocks:

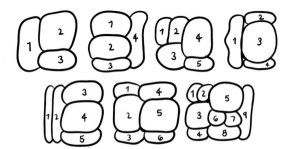

The glyph blocks are also read from left to right and from top to bottom. The difference is that the blocks are organized into paired columns. You scan them this way:

THE ROYAL ONTARIO MUSEUM
AND THE WORLD OF THE MAYA

Excavating a building sequence, 9th to 12th century CE, in the "Ottawa" plaza-courtyard group at Lamanai

The Royal Ontario Museum's role in the land of the ancient and modern Maya covers more than half a century. The story begins in the late 1950s when the Museum began to look beyond its traditional involvement in the archaeology of the Middle East and the Classical world. As is true of so many long-term projects, the birth of the ROM's engagement with the Maya world came not from a detailed plan but from a chance encounter between Kenneth Kidd, at the time curator of Ethnology at the ROM,

and A. H. Anderson, the first Archaeological Commissioner of Belize (then known, until 1973, as British Honduras). The meeting happened neither in Canada nor in Belize but in England, during an International Congress of Americanists. Surely neither of them knew, as Anderson spoke of his country's need for archaeological exploration and Kidd thought of his museum's hope to expand its archaeological role, how far-reaching the effects of their talk would become.

The first flowering of the ROM's new enterprise came when Dr. William Bullard joined the staff for the express purpose of developing a program of research in Belize. The country was almost a blank on the archaeological map of the southern Maya Lowlands, although work under the aegis of England's Royal Anthropological Institute took place in the 1920s, Sir J. Eric S. Thompson carried out excavations for the Carnegie Institution of Washington in the 1930s, and the early 1950s saw Harvard University enter the field for a time. The nature of archaeological funding, coupled with immense logistical difficulties, kept all the work at a relatively small scale; the ROM's hope was for a project that would span several seasons and operate on a moderately large scale. Bullard's first visit to Belize in 1961 was to set the stage for such an expedition, but the ever-present logistical problems and the arrival of Hurricane Hattie forced a change in plans. He carried out two small excavations, keeping his eye on the chance for a larger endeavour, but the main project proved impossible to kick into life. By the end of 1962, with Bullard's departure from the ROM, the Museum's prospects for major involvement seemed destined for the shelf.

Once again, chance intervened. While attending a meeting of the Society for American Archaeology in 1963, Kidd sat in on a session on fieldwork in Latin America and listened to a paper presented by David Pendergast, who had carried out work in one of Belize's caves earlier that year.

The jade head from Altun Ha, Tomb B-4/7, 14.9 cm high

After the session Kidd approached Pendergast, identified himself quite correctly as the only other person there with a connection to "British Honduras," and began a conversation that ended with a question: would Pendergast be interested in reviving the ROM's project in the country? Focused on his cave work, Pendergast replied rather noncommittally, but later that year, when a specific approach arrived from the Museum, he leapt at the chance.

In discussions with Kidd, and then with Dr. A. D. Tushingham, the ROM's Chief Archaeologist, Pendergast

Flaked stone in the shape of animals and a man, from Altun Ha tombs

Altun Ha polychrome bowl, c. 600 CE

promoted the idea of beginning work at a site he had tested during the summer, some 50 kilometres north of the country's capital, Belize City, and hence easier of access than other possible choices. It was agreed that work would begin as 1964 opened, and as the equipment amassed by Bullard had remained in Belize, the start-up was seen as a relatively easy one. Like almost every aspect of the work, appearances were deceptive, but before long the project was well under way. Pendergast christened the site "Altun Ha," which is a rendering in Yucatec Mayan of the name of the nearby local community, Rockstone

Pond. Altun Ha was to be the focus of a four-year excavation program, but as the importance of the ancient community emerged, plans were extended, and in the end the work lasted for seven seasons, from 1964 through 1970.

Altun Ha is small, indeed almost tiny, in comparison with the great ancient Maya centres such as Tikal in Guatemala. Yet the richness of its tombs, as well as the profusion of offerings cached beneath floors of successive buildings or included in burials throughout the site, belies its size. Of the many carved jades for which the site has become famous in Maya studies, the most outstanding are a massive jade plaque adorned with a ruler's image and a text in Mayan hieroglyphs, and the massive jade head known throughout Belize as the Sun God, *Kin'ich Ahau* although epigraphers now claim it represents a deity called the Jester God, who is a patron of rulership. The jade head has become a cultural icon in Belize, and appears on the country's stamps and currency. The importance of Altun Ha goes far beyond such objects, however; in a great many respects, the work at Altun Ha opened a window on life in the southern Maya Lowlands between about 800 BCE and 900 CE that had gone unrecognized until then. It remains among the richest sites of its size ever discovered in the Maya world.

With the Altun Ha project completed, Pendergast turned his attention to the site of Indian Church, as it was then known, some 40 kilometres to the west, and in 1974 a new expedition was under way. From the outset it was apparent, owing to the presence of the ruins of the church, that the site offered opportunities for broadening the picture of Maya life beyond what had emerged at Altun Ha. Because no religion establishes a church where there are no parishioners, the ruins suggested that the site might have been occupied through the centuries following the collapse of cities such as Altun Ha. The first bit of excavation, far north of the church, strengthened that suggestion, and before the first season ended there was convincing evidence that Indian Church had survived the collapse and continued to

The Jaguar Temple, Str. N10-9, at Lamanai

be an important focus of activity in the following centuries, and that it was still a functioning community when the Spaniards arrived in the sixteenth century. The site's new name of "Lamanai" is an approximation of the original Mayan name of the community, taken from lists of towns and villages in Belize drawn up by Spanish chroniclers.

Work at Lamanai continued under Pendergast's direction through 1986, and although the site has a substantial Preclassic and Classic period presence (c. 600 BCE–800 CE), it is best

David Pendergast reconstructing a large incense burner in the lab at Lamanai

Excavating a Late Classic building in the Ottawa Group

known for evidence of occupation continuity through the Maya collapse to the Spanish and British colonial periods (800 CE through to the 1860s). The significance of the site, and the huge quantity of structures left unexamined when the initial project ended, argued in favour of further exploration. Having worked at the site from 1983 through 1986 with Pendergast, Elizabeth Graham initiated a new phase of investigation in 1998. Since then, work at Lamanai has concentrated on critical periods of transition, such as the Classic collapse and the early Spanish colonial period, as well as on expanding access both to on-site collections and to the information derived from the archaeological work. From its roots as a ROM endeavour, the project is now multi-national with participants from institutions in Canada, Belize, Mexico, England, Scotland, France, and the United States.

The year 1986 also saw the start of work by Pendergast

The Tipu town centre, c. 1600. Painting by Marianne Huston

Chichén Itzá–style vase, Marco Gonzalez. 800–1000 CE

Guatemalan plumbate vessel, from Marco Gonzalez. 800–1000 CE

and Graham at a small but surprisingly rich site called Marco Gonzalez, situated at the southern tip of Belize's Ambergris Caye, one of the islands that dot the country's barrier reef. Work there has revealed the complex history of a sea-oriented community that served as a trading hub as well as a location for the production of salt. The strength of its ties to particular mainland centres in the Maya world change through time, but what remains constant is that Ambergris Caye communities were highly resilient. They were part of a coastal culture with its own dynamic, based on waterborne trade and communication that extended from modern Honduras to Tabasco. Marco Gonzalez, for example, reflected Peten spheres of influence in the Late Classic Period, Chichén Itzá and its trade activities in the Terminal Classic, Lamanai's florescence in the Early and Middle Post-Classic, and the transformations that characterized coastal commerce from Tabasco to Honduras in the Late Post-Classic and early Contact periods.

Closely related to Lamanai, owing to the presence of

Spanish mission churches at both communities, the site of Tipu also yielded evidence regarding Maya life in the 16th and 17th centuries. Tipu maintained strong connections with Lamanai during the Spanish colonial period, and is also important because it maintained ties with the rebellious communities of the Itzá and Kowoj, on the Peten Lakes, who never accepted Christianity.

The additions to the understanding of the Maya past that stem from the ROM's involvement have been many and varied, and they are recognized and utilized by all who seek to shed light on Maya cultural heritage. Beyond all this, however, lies a contribution of equal, if not greater, importance, though it is far less tangible. Near the halfway point of the Lamanai excavations, as work was being carried out on Structure N10-43, now known as the High Temple, and the tallest structure at the site, the Maya men on whom the project depended so heavily were lightening their workload with banter in Spanish, as always, while Pendergast stood nearby sorting out some stratigraphy. The conversation turned to the Mayan roots of the name "Lamanai." From that, Pendergast jumped to other site names, including one from far northern Yucatan which includes the surname of one of the men in the group. The others immediately began ragging the chap about how far he had fallen below the level of his ancestors, when suddenly the chatter ceased and one of the younger men, never a leader in such exchanges, stood up

to speak. Hesitating a bit at first, he expressed the thanks of the group, and of all the men, for the work that had gone on—not because it had given them employment and the means to better their lives in a material way, but because it had given them pride in being Maya. Surely no better result could be hoped for from the ROM's half-century of work.

Note:

In addition to the ROM sponsorship of the excavations mentioned above, work in Belize was made possible by grants from the Social Sciences and Humanities Research Council of Canada, the Richard Ivey Foundation of London, Ontario, the National Geographic Society, the Tinker Foundation, and York University. Work in recent years has been supported by the British Academy, FAMSI (Foundation for the Advancement of Mesoamerican Studies, Inc.), the Institute of Archaeology, University College London, and the University of London Central Research Fund. Development and community projects at Lamanai have been supported by the Canadian Fund for Local Initiatives (Canadian International Development Agency), the British High Commission Small Grants Fund, the Inter-American Development Bank Tourism Development Project, the U.S. Embassy, Andante Travel U.K., and ENCRyM (Escuela Nacional de Conservación, Restauración y Museografía de Instituto Nacional de Antropología e Historia, México).

EXHIBITION PROGRAMS

THE WILLIAM THORSELL FORUM

Collapse: How Societies Choose to Fail or Succeed
with Jared Diamond
Tuesday, November 1, 2011, 7–8:30 pm
$29/ROM Members $26

Speaker: Jared Diamond, author of the Pulitzer Prize–winning *Guns, Germs and Steel* and *Collapse*, is currently a professor of geography at UCLA. Diamond is also the author of two other best-selling books, *The Third Chimpanzee* and *Why Is Sex Fun?*

DISTINGUISHED LECTURER SERIES

Individual lectures:
$23/ROM Members $21
Lecture package (all 6 lectures for the price of 4):
$92/ROM Members $84

The Rise and Fall of the Sacred Rulers of the Maya World
with Justin Jennings
Tuesday, November 15, 2011, 7–8 pm

Justin Jennings is Curator, New World Archaeology, Royal Ontario Museum, and the lead curator of the ROM's exhibition *Maya: Secrets of their Ancient World*. He is currently completing analysis of a Middle Horizon mortuary cave (600–1000 CE). His recent books include *Globalizations and the Ancient World*, *Beyond Wari Walls*, and *Drink, Power, and Society in the Ancient Andes*.

What Not to Believe About the Ancient Maya
with Elizabeth Graham
Tuesday, November 22, 2011, 7–8 pm

Elizabeth Graham is a professor at the Institute of Archaeology, University College, London, and an adjunct research professor in anthropology at the University of Western Ontario. Her recent book, *Maya Christians and Their Churches in Sixteenth-Century Belize,* is centred on the Spanish *visita* missions at Tipu and Lamanai.

The Terminal Classic Period in the Northern Maya Lowlands: New Perspectives on the City of Sayil and the Puuc Region
with Jeremy A. Sabloff
Tuesday, December 6, 2011, 7–8 pm

Jeremy A. Sabloff is the author or editor of more than 20 books and monographs, such as *Archaeology Matters*, *The New Archaeology and the Ancient Maya*, *Cities of Ancient Mexico*, and *A History of American Archaeology* (with Gordon R. Willey), as well as countless chapters and articles on the Maya and the history of archaeology.

Reconsidering Ideas about Early Maya Political Organization
with Helen R. Haines
Tuesday, January 31, 2012, 7–8 pm

Helen R. Haines is a research associate at the Archaeological Research Centre, Trent University, and teaches in the university's Department of Anthropology and at the University of Toronto Mississauga. She is currently director of the Ka'Kabish Archaeological Research Project in north-central Belize.

Palenque: The Art and History of an Ancient Maya Royal Court
with David Stuart
Tuesday, February 28, 2012, 7–8 pm

In 2004 David Stuart was appointed as the Linda and David Schele Professor of Mesoamerican Art and Writing at the University of Texas at Austin. His publications include *Ten Phonetic Syllables* and *Corpus of Maya Hieroglyphic Inscriptions*. Stuart is also the director of the Mesoamerica Center at UT Austin.

The End of Time: The Maya Mystery of 2012
with Anthony Aveni
Tuesday, March 20, 2012, 7–8 pm

Anthony Aveni is the Russell B. Colgate Professor of Astronomy and Anthropology, serving appointments in both the Department of Physics and Astronomy and the Department of Sociology and Anthropology at Colgate University, Hamilton, New York. Dr. Aveni helped develop the field of archaeoastronomy and now is considered one of the founders of Mesoamerican archaeoastronomy, in particular for his research in the astronomical history of the Maya people of ancient Mexico. Dr. Aveni is a lecturer, speaker, and editor/author of more than two dozen books on ancient astronomy.

COURSE

The Maya World
Instructor: Erin Kerr
Saturdays, January 21 to February 25, 2012, 1:30–3:30 pm (6 weeks)
$180/ROM Members $160

Kings and queens, forgotten cities, spectacular temples, and bloody rituals are all hallmarks of the Classic Maya Period (250–900 CE). Explore one of the world's most enigmatic ancient civilizations with hands-on materials and a guided tour of the ROM's exhibition *Maya: Secrets of their Ancient World*.

Erin Kerr is a teacher in the ROM Education Department.

Royal Ontario Museum
100 Queen's Park
Toronto, Ontario M5S 2C6
www.rom.on.ca

Library and Archives Canada Cataloguing in Publication

Jennings, Justin–
    Maya: Secrets of their ancient world / Justin Jennings, Martha Cuevas García and Roberto López Bravo

Guide to accompany the exhibition held at the Royal Ontario Museum, Toronto, Ont., Nov. 19, 2011–Apr. 9, 2012.
ISBN 978-0-88854-487-2
    1. Mayas—Exhibitions. I. Cuevas García, Martha II. López Bravo, Roberto III. Title.

F1435.J46 2011   972.81'016074713541   C2011-906474-X

Justin Jennings is Curator of New World Archaeology at the Royal Ontario Museum.

Martha Cuevas García is an Investigator of the National Institute of Anthropology and History (INAH) and has directed archaeological fieldwork at the site of Palenque for the last 16 years.

Roberto López Bravo is Director of the Regional Museum of Tuxtla Gutiérrez and a Professor in the School of Archaeology in the Science and Arts University of Chiapas.

David Pendergast, Curator Emeritus in the Department of World Cultures at the Royal Ontario Museum, is the former director of the Lamanai Archaeological Project, and has worked in Belize since the late 1950s. He is also an Honorary Research Fellow at the Institute of Archaeology, University College of London.

Elizabeth Graham is Professor of Mesoamerican Archaeology at the Institute of Archaeology, University College London, and Adjunct Research Professor in Anthropology at the University of Western Ontario.

Project Director: Glen Ellis; Editor: Andrea Gallagher Ellis; Design: Meagan Durlak, Tara Winterhalt; Project Assistant: Sheeza Sarfraz

Cover photos: Incense-burner stand depicting the Jaguar God of the Underworld (detail). Ceramic, Late Classic (600–900 CE). Comitán, Chiapas, Mexico. Museo Regional de Chiapas. Image © CONACULTA.-INAH.-MEX. Jorge Vertiz 2011. Reproduction authorized by the National Institute of Anthropology and History. Temple photograph: Ariadne Van Zandbergen / www.africaimagelibrary.com

The Royal Ontario Museum and the Canadian Museum of Civilization would like to thank the following institutions and museums for generously lending artifacts to this exhibition. Mexico: CONACULTA - Instituto Nacional de Antropología e Historia (INAH), Centro INAH Campeche, Museo Arqueológico de Campeche Fuerte de San Miguel, and Museo del Camino Real de Hecelchakán, State of Campeche; Museo Regional de Yucatán Palacio Cantón and Museo de Sitio Chichén Itzá, State of Yucatán; Museo de Sitio de Comalcalco and Museo de Sitio Pomoná, State of Tabasco; Museo Regional de Tuxtla Gutiérrez, Museo de Sitio de Palenque Alberto Ruz L'huillier, Museo de Sitio Toniná and Proyecto arqueológico Crecimiento Urbano de Palenque, State of Chiapas; Museo Regional de Antropología Carlos Pellicer Cámara of the Instituto de Cultura de Tabasco, Museo Ventura Martín Azcuaga, State of Tabasco; Museo Amparo, State of Puebla; U.S.A: The Cleveland Museum of Art, Cleveland; Dumbarton Oaks, Washington, DC; Hudson Museum, The University of Maine, Orono; Kimbell Art Museum, Fort Worth; The Metropolitan Museum of Art, New York; Princeton University Art Museum, Princeton; Canada: Gardiner Museum, Toronto; U.K: The British Museum, London.

Photos: Brian Boyle, pp. 25, 27, 57, 64, 65, 68; British Museum, p. 36; The Cleveland Museum of Art, p. 48; Dumbarton Oaks, p. 45; Painting by Marianne Huston: 68; Justin Kerr, p. 45; Lamanai Archaeological Project, 63, 66, 67; Jorge Pérez de Lara, pp. 20, 33, 35, 47, 56; Princeton University Art Museum, pp. 30, 32; Jorge Vértiz, pp. 19, 21–24, 26, 28–29, 31, 34, 37–39, 42–44, 46, 50–53; Medioimages/Photodisc, p.13; Michel Zabé, p. 55

Printed and bound in Canada by MIL, an RR Donnelley Plant, Toronto, Ontario

The Royal Ontario Museum is an agency of the Government of Ontario.